OREGON'S GREAT TRAIN HOLDUP

Southern Pacific Company
(PACIFIC SYSTEM)

REWARD

This Company will, as to each person who participated in the hold-up of our Train No. 13, at Tunnel 13 near Siskiyou, Jackson County, Oregon, at about 12:40 P. M., Thursday, October 11, 1923, pay a reward of $2500 for information directly leading to arrest and conviction.

First of millions of "WANTED" posters appears same day as the train holdup. (below) Burned out Railway Post Office car on siding at Ashland several days after the car was dynamited and the mail clerk inside the car was killed and cremated.

OREGON'S GREAT TRAIN HOLDUP

BANDITS MURDER 4—DIDN'T GET A DIME!

[Documentary] *10121595*

LAST GREAT TRAIN HOLDUP IN THE WEST

364.1552

BERT & MARGIE WEBBER

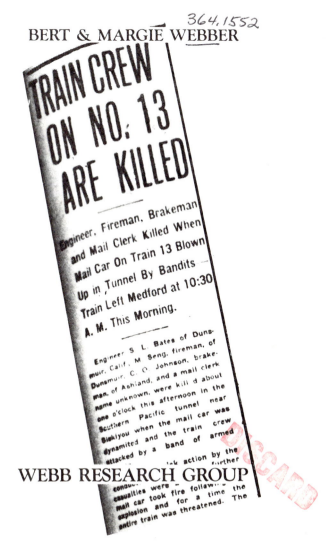

TRAIN CREW ON NO. 13 ARE KILLED

Engineer, Fireman, Brakeman and Mail Clerk Killed When Mail Car On Train 13 Blown Up in Tunnel By Bandits Train Left Medford at 10:30 A. M. This Morning.

Engineer S. L. Bates of Dunsmuir, Calif. M Seng, fireman, of Dunsmuir. C. O. Johnson, brakeman, of Ashland, and a mail clerk name unknown, were kill d about one o'clock this afternoon in the Southern Pacific tunnel near Siskiyou when the mail car was dynamited and the train crew attacked by a band of armed

k action by the further

consu___ casualties were — mail car took fire follow___ the explosion and for a time the entire train was threatened. The

WEBB RESEARCH GROUP

Published by: WEBB RESEARCH GROUP
Direct all inquiries to the distributor:

PACIFIC NORTHWEST BOOKS COMPANY
SAN 200-5263
P.O. Box 314   Medford, Oregon 97501

LIBRARY OF CONGRESS
Cataloging in Publications Data

Webber, Bert
    Oregon's great train holdup [bandits murder 4—didn't get a dime!]
    Bibliography: p.
    Includes index.
    1. Train robberies—Oregon [2. DeAutremont, Hugh. 3. DeAutremont, Ray. 4. DeAutremont, Roy. 5. Holdup of Southern Pacific train no. 13, October 11, 1923] I. Webber, Margie II. Title
HV6661.072W43 1988   364.1'552'097925   88-27785
ISBN 0-936738-31-6

Table of Contents

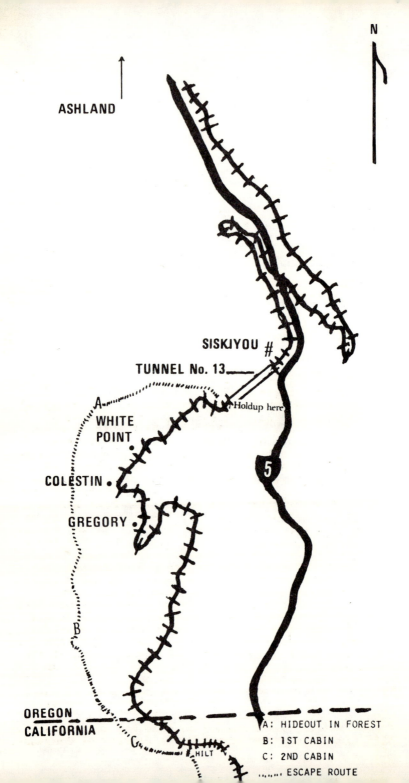

N

ASHLAND

SISKIYOU #

TUNNEL No. 13

Holdup here

WHITE POINT

COLESTIN

GREGORY

5

OREGON
CALIFORNIA

HILT

A: HIDEOUT IN FOREST
B: 1ST CABIN
C: 2ND CABIN
.......: ESCAPE ROUTE

Introduction

Shortly after the De Autremont brothers were sent to spend the remainder of their lives in the Oregon State Penitentiary in 1927, a leather-bound gold-stamped "souvenier" picture album was released by the U.S. Post Office. Its title:

Story of the Holdup of Southern Pacific Train No. 13, October 23, 1923—Capture and Conviction of the De Autremont Brothers.

Copies of this album were eagerly sought ·by rail-roaders and others who had known the victims. Many public libraries as well as museums and railroad historians desired copies but exactly to whom the distribution was made will probably never be known, especially now over 60 years later. Nevertheless, hundreds of people who wanted copies did not receive any. Rare book dealers shrug their shoulders when asked about this unique item. One of the original albums was made available to us in 1973 through the cooperation of then chief postal inspector William J. Cotter, United States Postal Service, Washington, D.C. This was coordinated by Nolan R. Brown, Postal Inspector in Charge, Seattle, Washington, and Steve J. Schneringer, Postal Inspector at Medford, Oregon. Gentlemen: Everyone reading this book thanks you. Ye Galleon Press published a small 50th Anniversary edition of selected material from the album in 1973. It quickly sold out. In 1974 we added some new data for an expanded edition. That 32-page booklet was very popular and remained on sale through mid-1988. Final copies were removed from sale to make room for this new much larger book on the occasion of the 65th anniversary of this infamous holdup and murders.

In order to make this book as meaningful as possible, we have now added more material, much of which has come our way since the 1974 edition. One will note we have retained the main title, *Oregon's Great Train Holdup*, but expanded on this for fuller identification in cooperation with the Library of Congress.

We might say a few words about "robbery" and "holdup."

To have a robbery, as many term this event to have been, one must engage in "the felonious taking of the property of another...against his will...." (*Random House Dictionary of the English Language*.)

A definition of holdup is not as clearly stated with the implication that a "robbery" and a "holdup" might be one and the same act. The same source gives us for "holdup," "A stop or delay in the process of something ...a forcible stopping [a holdup]" and robbing a person or place. "Holdup" does not appear in *The Oxford Dictionary of English Etymology* but "rob" does: "to deprive by force; plunder, pillage." For our purpose here we consider this event in history as a "holdup" because nothing was taken.

We have been fortunate in reaching a number of retired trainmen who remembered the victims including one who was at the scene of the holdup as part of the first team to investigate the report of trouble at Siskiyou.

Mr. E. M. Hale, Southern Pacific Transportation Company, Dunsmuir, California, filled in names and locations of long since discontinued sidings in the area of the blowing up of the mail car. And we appreciated the assistance given before his retirement of Robert A. Sederholm, of the public relations department of SP in San Francisco.

To Richard J. Portal, in 1973 head of reference department, Jackson County Library System, and to his assistants, and to the present staff of reference librarians headed by Anne Billeter, we tip our hats for invaluable bibliographic service.

Some of the items in this book may be seen in the permanent exhibit in the museum of the Southern Oregon Historical Society in Jacksonville, Oregon. This is a public museum occupying the former Court House where the trial was held.

Many thanks to James Long and his editors, for use of material from Jim's article, "Sensational Train Robber Finally Off Parole," in *Oregon Journal*, November 17, 1972.

We are indebted to the management of the Medford *Mail Tribune* for access to the 1923 issues of the paper and for permission to use some clips from that paper here.

We are also pleased to have had the assistance of our sons Dale B. and Lauren T. Webber. They went on field trips, especially to Tunnel 13 and who worked in the photo lab with picture processing.

The photographs in this book were selected from

the original album unless otherwise credited.

Some years ago we had a letter from Chester Silliman who in 1923 was a teenaged National Guardsman called, among others, to stand guard at Tunnel 13 the night of the trouble there. We met with him in the fall of 1988 when he told of his recollections. Chet is now in his eighties.

Appreciating the fact that many of today's younger readers don't know what an "Oh-3 Springfield" rifle is, or a government issue Colt .45 automatic, we sought examples of these weapons in order to present current photographs. Medford gunsmith Bob Kennedy provided the rifle with sling. We asked the Oregon National Guard about a Colt .45 automatic and Supply Sergeant Johnny Meyer, "A" Company, 186th Infantry, produced one from his armory. These are the models mentioned in this book. We thank these men for their interest and help.

Not only is Karen Bolz Cramer an expert typist, she is an executive secretary and is our friend. She makes time for our typing needs and is an integral part of our team. In addition to thanking her, she also gets hugged!

While we have searched for accurate data for this book, there is wide variation in newspaper stories of the period and time fades memories of some of those who were on hand many decades ago. We trust this book will find favor with the dwindling numbers of railroaders who were working out of the Ashland and Dunsmuir yards in the early 1920s and will prove useful as a documentary of what happened, to the present generation of readers, in what has been termed "The Last Great Train Holdup of the West."

Bert and Margie Webber
Central Point, Oregon
October, 1988

The Last Great Train Holdup of the West

The greatest writer of mystery fiction could hardly have created a plot as confusing, a world-wide hunt as thrilling, a capture and trial as brilliant, as that which ended with the jailing of three brothers for holding up a train and murdering four men.

At about 12:40 p.m., Thursday, October 11, 1923, Southern Pacific Train No. 13 was emerging from Tunnel No. 13 in the Siskiyou Mountains of Oregon. The train was suddenly forced to stop by armed men. Their plan was to rob the Railway Post Office car of $40,000 they believed was carried in the car.

The marauders shot and killed a brakeman, the engineer and the fireman. They dynamited the mail car thus killing the mail clerk. The trio obtained no loot. It was much later when they learned that the car held only a usual run of mail and express.

Post Office Inspectors and Special Agents of the Southern Pacific Company were immediately called to the scene. Sheriff's posses and National Guard troops were sent to comb the mountains. Railroad men, on learning of the murders, formed their own posses. One of these men, in 1973 in his 80's, when interviewed, turned toward Siskiyou Summit and declared: "...and if we'd caught those fellows we wouldn't have brought them back alive!" But the plunderers had fled.

After an investigation which included scientific analysis of evidence, authorities concluded that the crimes had been committed by Roy and Ray De Autremont, twin brothers 23 years of age, and their brother Hugh De Autremont, 19. Warrants for their arrests were issued. Rewards posted within hours of the holdup were increased, but the three young desperados were not to be found. It appeared the only way they would be found was through the publication of their photographs. Because of an alert criminologist, the men's identity was determined. As soon as their pictures were obtained, over two-and-one-half million "WANTED"

Baldwin locomotive No. 3629 pulled train No. 13 on October 11, 1923. Although this engine was not damaged in dynamite blast, both the engineer and fireman were murdered. No.3629 served the SP until 1956 when it was scrapped.

circulars, many bearing their pictures, and some even with hand writing samples, were distributed. These posters were sent throughout the United States as well as over seas. These were published in English, Spanish, French, German, Dutch and Portugese.

Many newspaper reporters, seeing this event to be worthy of feature articles, wrote pieces for newspapers and magazines in all sections of the United States. For illustrations they used the men's photographs and a spectacular picture of the exploded end of the mail car.

One of the "WANTED" posters was on a bulletin board at the army camp on Angel Island in San Francisco Bay. In early July 1926, on the 2nd in fact, Army Sergeant Thomas Reynolds went to the Southern Pacific office in San Francisco. Sergeant Reynolds would only speak "with the man in charge," so was ushered into the office of William H. Stone, SP Agent for San Francisco. The sergeant identified the man in the poster as one Private James C. Price of B Company, 31st Infantry who was on foreign service in the Philippine Islands under this assumed name. Reynolds qualified that he knew Price as Price had been in his outfit.

Investigations take time and this one was no exception. Months dragged by when, finally in November 1926, railroad Inspector Fred Smith took ship to Manila to seek out Private Price.

By early February Smith's investigations were complete and it was announced that James C. Price, was the alias of Hugh De Autremont who with his two brothers was wanted in Oregon for murdering a train crew and the blowing up of a United States Railway Post Office car.

About a month later, when the ship docked in San Francisco, Hugh was transferred to Alcatraz Island Disciplinary Barracks. Under close questioning, Hugh admitted his identity but disclaimed all knowledge as to the whereabouts of his brothers.

The yard east of Tunnel 13 at Siskiyou Station. This is a single track tunnel 3,107.70 feet long. The Siskiyou branch carries only freight, passenger service being by way of Klamath Falls to eliminate the tight and steep turns in the Siskiyou Mountains.

Some time later, one of the many feature news stories was published in Ohio, complete with pictures of the two still at-large brothers. The men were spotted and quickly arrested in Stubenville where they had adopted the name "Goodwin." In Ohio, Ray had married Hazel Sprouse. The two became parents with the birth of Jackie Hugh Goodwin [De Autremont]. When Roy and Ray were extradited to Oregon, Ray was forced to leave his wife and son behind.

Recalling the events of the tragedy in 1973, a retired railroad engineer said he felt lucky to be alive because just weeks before the holdup and murders, he had been fireman for engineer Sidney L. Bates on Train No. 13. The former trainman said he had been moved to the "engineer's list" and young Marvin L. Seng had taken his place. Both Bates and Seng were murdered.

Freight train headed by three diesel units emerges from East
Portal, Tunnel 13, at Siskiyou Station 4,130 feet altitude.
Trains stop here for break check before descending into the
Rogue Valley.

The now white-haired railroader (who requested
that his name not be used for publication) was, on
that day in 1923, the engineer on a work-train. His
train had been chugging up the west side of the mountain, but was switched onto the Gregory siding below
the tunnel to clear the track for the San Francisco
Express (Train No. 13). "The explosion shook the
earth for miles," he recalled. Men on his train as
well as those at Siskiyou Station at the east end of
the tunnel, thought the boiler on No. 13 had blown.

As to how the train happened to be going so slowly
to allow two of the bandits to board at Siskiyou—
then what happened and who called for help, has been
pieced together following interviews with several
former as well as present trainmen, and a look at old
newspapers. We also studied the railroad gradient chart.

The grade to Siskiyou is quite steep on both sides
of the tunnel. From Ashland yard to Siskiyou Station,
the grade averages 2.46 percent with the steepest at

3.1 percent between mileposts 421 and 422. The top is
4,130 feet elevation at milepost 412. Heading toward
California, the grade approaches the top at 2.7 percent,
levels out for a very short distance then plunges into
the tunnel at the rate of 2 percent downgrade. The
average grade from the summit to Hilt, in California,
(MP 402) is 2.04 percent with the steepest (3.1 percent)
between MP 405-406 but there is a 3 percent near the
old White Point siding (tracks now removed) between MP
409-410. These grades are the steepest on all of the
Southern Pacific system.* The climb to Siskiyou Station
from either side has always required more than a single
engine—"helpers." These were wood or coal-burners in
the early days then oil-fired steam locomotives at the
time of this holdup. Today: diesels. Very many years
ago there was a turntable at Siskiyou thus helper engines assigned to Ashland and to Dunsmuir divisions
stopped at the summit, turned around and went back to
their own yards.

It was policy that all trains test brakes while
at Siskiyou before starting down mountain in either
direction. Having watched train operations there
many times, while ploting their crime, the De Autremonts came up with a scheme whereby this break-
checking activity would become their access to the
train.

The men had earlier found an abandoned cabin in
the forest to hide food and in which to live as they
made final plans. They carried several guns. There
were three .45 hand guns, one an army automatic, the
others believed to be revolvers. They also had a
repeating shotgun and Roy pocketed a blackjack.

On the day for their "action," Ray had stationed
himself at the west portal. He had the shotgun and
a .45 pistol. He also had dynamite and a stolen
detonator with which to blow open the mail car door.
The plan was for the robbery to happen at the west
portal. Hugh and Roy had hidden themselves near the
track in bushes at east portal.

After Train No. 13, which was officially named
"The San Francisco Express," arrived from Ashland,
dropped the "helper" and tested brakes, it was ready
for the down-hill grade. When the train left Siskiyou,
its speed might pick up to five or six miles an hour
before it reached the tunnel, about one hundred yards

---

* Although some writers have declared the SP's Siskiyou line to
be the steepest grade in the nation, the Association of American
Railroads says the steepest known grade on a line-haul railroad
is 5.89 percent near Madison, Indiana. On the main line of a
line-haul railroad 4.7 percent is in the Blue Ridge Mountains in
North Carolina.

.45 Colt automatic found near east end of tunnel where it had been dropped by bandit in his scurry to climb aboard the train. See filed off serial number but gun bore secret number and was later traced to one of the De Autremont brothers.

along the track. Roy and Hugh were to jump aboard the tender as the locomotive entered the tunnel. It was almost touch-and-go! Hugh raced to the train and reaching it before Roy, Hugh climbed on. Roy was still chugging along as the train picked up speed but in the sudden exercise, Roy's pistol fell out of his belt to the ground. Roy seems to have slowed momentarily as if thinking whether he should fetch the gun or go on without it. He left the gun where it fell. But the train was going faster. Realizing that Roy could no longer reach the hand-hold on the tender, Hugh stuck out his foot which Roy was able to grab, then Roy pulled himself up to the car.

Hugh and Roy, after catching their breaths for only a few seconds, climbed over the tender and dropped into the engine's cab. As they did so, Hugh poked his pistol at engineer Sid Bates yelling above the noise of the locomotive in the close-quarters of the tunnel to stop the train just as the engine cleared the portal. Realizing he had no choice, Bates closed his throttle and hit the air brakes which brought the train to a stop just as the loco-

Two of the De Autremont boys hopped aboard the tender then scrambled into the cab in the dark of the tunnel where they surprised the engineer and the fireman then forced the engineer to stop the train.

motive left the tunnel. The two bandits told fireman Marv Seng and engineer Bates to leave the engine and to go stand on the track at the front end. In the meantime Ray, who had been at the west portal all this time, appeared with the shotgun and Roy told him he'd lost his pistol while trying to get on the tender. Ray gave him his.

Some reports suggest the door on the mail car opened slightly and the clerk, Elvyn E. Dougherty, took a peek to see what all the comotion was about. Apparently Ray blasted at the mail car with the shotgun which caused Dougherty to shut and lock the door. The Railway Post Office car was still inside the tunnel. Ray, whose job it was to handle the dynamite, went for the suitcase in which the dynamite had been carried to the scene and handed the suitcase to Roy. Roy piled the explosive at the car's door then he raced for the detonator. He pushed the detonator's handle as far as it would go.. The resulting explosion was horrendous—too much dynamite—which not only blew up the end of the steel mail car but ruptured the air and steam lines. The explosion killed the mail clerk and started a fire inside the car.

Was there a witness? Hugh Haffley, the baggage

Type of Nash touring car used by De Autremont brothers during tour of Oregon seeking place to plunder. Was also used for a quick trip away from the hideout to obtain supplies.

tender, wondered about the train's sudden stop and most quietly opened his door and very cautiously, but without knowing why the need for caution, spied the bandits with guns aimed at the crew. He most quietly closed his door. He locked it. He sat tight. He was later knocked unconscious by the explosion but he survived.

After the explosion, the plan called for uncoupling the mail car from the train and ordering the engineer to pull the car out of the tunnel. Hugh De Autremont ordered Bates to move the train.

Roy and his twin Ray peered into the mail car but could see nothing due to the smoke, burning mail and leaking live steam. After a few seconds, Roy went to the back of the mail car to see about unhooking it. He was surprised to see a form walking in the tunnel carrying a red lantern. It was brakeman Coyl Johnson. Johnson had come forward to determine why the train had stopped in the tunnel and was probably of the opinion that the thunderous explosion had been caused by the blowing up of the boiler. Johnson was told, at the point of a pistol, that the mail car was being held up and he, Johnson, was to help unhook the car. Johnson stammered that it would only be possible to break the coupling if the locomotive pulled the car ahead slightly while the pin was lifted.

Coyl Johnson, still carrying his red lantern, was told to make his way through the dusty air of the tunnel to the locomotive. There, he came upon Ray and Hugh who were surprised to see him. Ray had seen someone coming with a red light. Ray was quoted in the *Newsletter* of the Postal Inspection Service in 1973 where he said:

> I shot at this man with my shotgun and at the same
> time Hugh shot him with his .45 Colt. The man

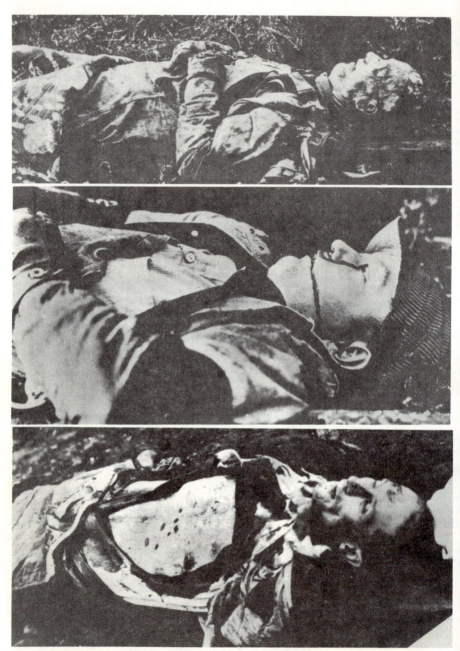

From top: Engineer Sidney L. Bates, Dunsmuir, California, was killed when shot by Hugh with the .45 Colt. Fireman Marvin L. Seng, Dunsmuir, was killed by Roy. Brakeman Coyl A. Johnson Ashland, was blasted by Ray with the shotgun then was shot again by Hugh's automatic.

The U.S. mail clerk on Train No. 13 was Elvyn E. Dougherty. He was killed as a result of the exolosion then cremated in the fire that followed. The coroner was of the opinion that the bones (arrow) are Dougherty's vertebrae.

Burned out mail car at White Point siding
before it was hauled to the Ashland yard.

> staggered. [I could see] he was dying and either
> Hugh or I shot him again.

Johnson fell to the ground saying something about
the other fellow (Roy) had told him to tell the men up
front to move the train ahead. Coyl A. Johnson died
right there.

The engineer was put back into the cab and Hugh
yelled to him to pull the mail car ahead. Ray continued:

> [The engineer] attempted to do this a number of
> times but the engine wheels merely spun and [the
> cars] failed to move. Hugh then put the engineer
> back on the ground beside the fireman while Roy
> and I looked the thing over to see what would be
> done [about] uncoupling the mail car and engine, but
> we...could not move either.

When the story got out later about the engine being
slugged to a stop, on the demands of the bandits, an
old timer engineer contended that enginner Sydney
Bates had a nickname of "hydraulic Sid." Whenever
Bates brought his train to a stop he "big holed" the
brakes completely filling the air retaining tanks so
there was no way the train could move "even an inch"
while passengers were entering or leaving the cars.
With high pressure air in the tanks, an engineer knew
he had to wait a few minutes—one or two minutes any-
way—for the pressure to decay before the train would
move. Of course the bandits didn't know about this
so could have presumed Bates was stalling about moving
the train.

Interior of mail car as seen from blown-out end. (Below) Postal Inspectors and railroad officials look at damaged car then sought remains of mail. Mail that could be identified was forwarded or returned to senders. Note heavy saw-horse and block supporting end of the car.

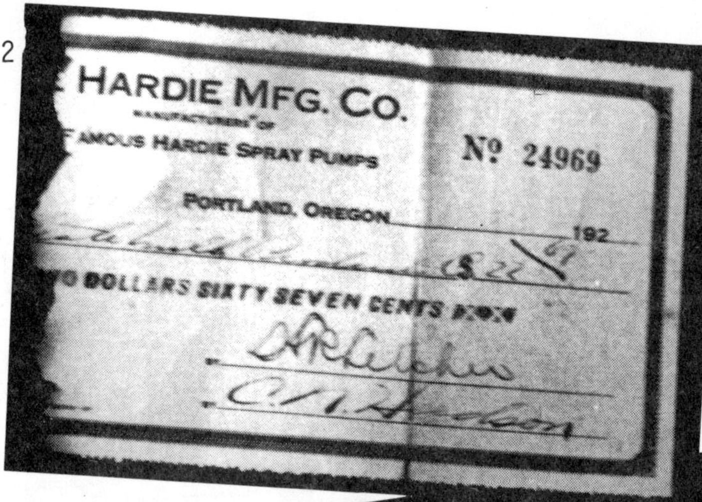

HARDIE MFG. CO.
MANUFACTURERS OF
FAMOUS HARDIE SPRAY PUMPS
No. 24969
PORTLAND, OREGON
192_

TWO DOLLARS SIXTY SEVEN CENTS $2.67

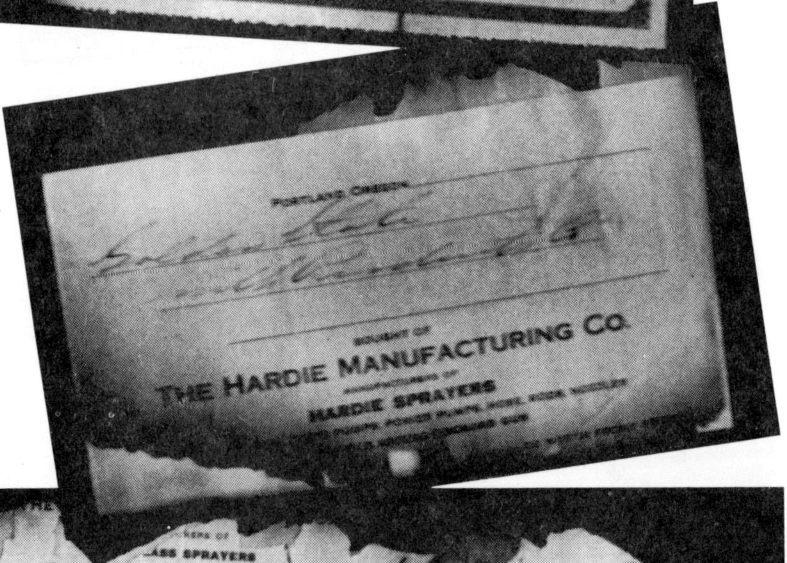

PORTLAND, OREGON

BOUGHT OF
THE HARDIE MANUFACTURING CO.
HARDIE SPRAYERS

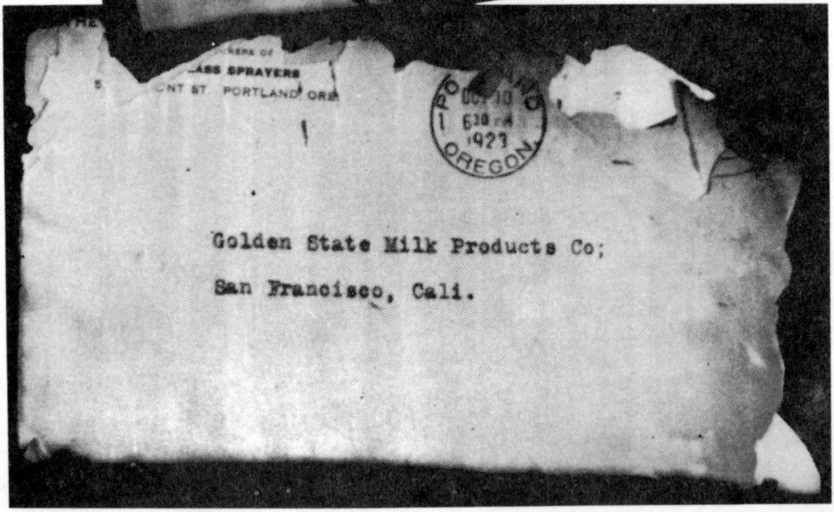

GLASS SPRAYERS
NT ST PORTLAND ORE

PORTLAND
OREGON
1927

Golden State Milk Products Co;
San Francisco, Cali.

There was a post office at Siskiyou, Oregon from April 6, 1895 until October 31, 1932 with mail being received and dispatched on the Railway Mail Service cars. Rail mail service clerk Dougherty picked up the bag from the Siskiyou postmaster as undoubtedly his last business before being blown up in the explosion of his mail car a few minutes later.

(Pictures page 22) The Hardie Manufacturing Company in Portland, Oregon did business with Golden State Milk Products Company in San Francisco, California. Hardie remitted its check No. 24969 for $22.67 and mailed this in an envelope that was postmarked, "Portland, Oregon, Oct. 10, 6:30 PM, 1923." This mail was damaged in the fire in the Railway Mail Service RPO car the next day as Train No. 13 passed through Tunnel No. 13 at Siskiyou summit.

Ray was further quoted:

Roy and I went back to the mail car and entered through the [blown out] front end. Our flashlights would not cut the steam and smoke [so we] left the mail car.
Hugh, in the meantime, had ordered the engineer back into the cab. The fireman [was] standing alongside the engine with his arms in the air. Roy and I held a brief consultation as to what to do. We decided to kill the fireman. Roy shot him twice with [the] Colt. Hugh had the engineer covered and I shouted at him to bump him off and [then] let's clear out. Hugh shot the engineer in the head with his Colt.

Post Office Department
Post Office
Official Business
(No. 84)

This mail damaged by fire and dynamite in hold-up of Ashland & Gerber Train No. 13, at Siskiyou, Oregon, October 11, 1923.

This letter was written October 9, 1923 then mailed and postmarked at McMinnville, Oregon on the 10th at 3:30 in the afternoon. Records are elusive whether this letter boarded Train No. 13 in Portland or when the train stopped in Salem. This letter, in its closed sack, was in the Railway Post Office car when the car was dynamited at Siskiyou on the 11th. The entire car load of damaged mail was sent (in new packaging) to the post office in San Francisco for salvage. Letter shown was forwarded under "penalty envelope" to addressee in Los Angeles Oct. 24th.

Remains of metal-banded wood shipping chest used by
the bandits for shipping their weapons used in the
holdup. Was burned, with trash, at forest hideout.
Identified by remnant of express address tag
found among ashes.

Frustration had truly set in for the brothers. The
debris in the mail car was so severe and the smoke so
heavy there seemed no way to sort our money they believed was in the car. The brothers were now stuck
with events they had not planned. The postal clerk,
Dougherty, had been blown up with the explosion and
his body consumed in the flash fire.
Realizing they had botched their job, the De Autremont brothers left the track and ran up the mountain
into the cover of the trees. The men were so confused
that at first they could not find their *cache*. Their
hideout was between two and three miles in a westerly
direction from the west end of the tunnel.
While the De Autremonts were leaving the scene,
Conductor Marrett and a passenger came out of the dark
tunnel to investigate the explosion they believed had
stopped the train. The two men were stunned at the
sight. Marrett went to an emergency phone near the
tunnel and reported to the agents at Ashland. In
turn, SP men called Jackson County Sheriff then a
call was made to Dan O'Connell, Chief Special Agent
at San Francisco.

TUNNEL 13
PICTURE
HISTORY
1923-1988
-65 YEARS-

(Left page) West Portal, Tunnel
No. 13, within minutes of disaster on Oct. 11, 1923. Track crews
were working before bodies of the
dead (arrow) were removed.
(Below, left) Tunnel as it appeared in November 1972.
(This page, top) Tunnel 13 as seen
in October 1988—65 years after
the crime. (Lower) In 1978 the
walls of the tunnel were blast-
treated with gunnite as a preservative. Inscription is of work
crew. In 1988, timber beams are
being replaced with steel inside
the tunnel.

View through West Portal of
Tunnel No. 13 from about
1-car length inside tunnel
about where mail car would
have been stopped when
blasted with dynamite.
(Below) Author Margie Webber
on research trip to West
Portal points to area where
corpses of dead trainmen
were placed by SP track
crew.

Not only did the explosion roar through the canyons
of the mountains, it brought life at Siskiyou Station
to a sudden unbelieveable momentary standstill. The
train had made an unscheduled stop in the tunnel and
smoke was now beginning to seep out the east portal
3,107.7 feet away from the blast. In an instant, those
at Siskiyou came to an unspoken decision: Rescue!
Steam was still up on the "helper" engine that was on
a side track. The crew, and extra men, raced into the
cab while switchmen turned the handle to route this
locomotive back onto the main line. Fresh air was
urgently needed for the dozens of passengers presently
trapped in the cars deep in the tunnel. The helper-
engine's headlight would hardly pierce the thick,
acrid smoke that had been dampened by the escaping
steam. The rescue locomotive rumbled through the tunnel slowly not wanting to crash the end of the stalled
train. In what was only seconds but seemed much
longer, faint red dots appeared in the gloom and grew
larger as the relief engine came upon the stopped
train—the two red oil lanterns one on each side of
the train's last car.

The helper engine's crew quickly coupled to the
end of the train and with a brief two-blasts of it's
whistle—the bare amount of steam permitted into the
whistle to almost not even blow the whistle because
of the confined space of the tunnel—the engine back-
ed the train out of the tunnel to the Siskiyou yard.
Here passengers literally tumbled from the cars gulp-
ing for fresh air. Passengers did not yet know what
was going on.

While the rescue engine was in the tunnel, some of
these trainmen ran to the west portal to investigate.
They were amazed to find the exploded mail car, the
engine and tender in apparent good shape (no exploded boiler) then one man found the lead wires which
had been used to set off the blast as another shouted
he had seen three corpses—the engine's crew and a
brakeman. Then they realized what had happened. The
mail car was still burning. Now, having been uncoup-
led from the rest of the train before the rescue engine pulled the passenger cars back to Siskiyou, a
relief engineer took Sid Bates' place in the cab of
the original locomotive, released brakes and slowly
pulled the blazing car down the mountain to the by-
pass track at White Point. White Point was two and
one-half miles below Siskiyou Station and about one
mile north of Colestin. All of these places on the
Oregon side of the state line.

The next day the now burned out Railway Post Office car was brought to the Southern Pacific yard at
Ashland where post office officials carefully looked

for what they expected to find—charred human bones
of their young red-headed mail clerk. There they were,
the remains of Elvyn E. Dougherty.

    *   *   *

  News of the disaster in the tunnel slowly but surely swept through the Rogue River Valley towns of Ashland, Talent, Phoenix, Medford and Central Point. It
took longer to reach Grants Pass. First word swept
through the railroad community of Ashland by word-of-
mouth. With the sheriff's office in Jacksonville,
five miles west of Medford, notified, the word got out
there. Somebody called the newspaper in Medford where
editors were in process of putting the evening paper
"to bed" with the lead story about Babe Ruth winning
a baseball game for the Yankees. It was a "dead" news
day until whomever put down the telephone and raced
into the editor's office with the startling news of
the train holdup, explosion and murders.
  The front page was re-platted for a banner headline

4 KILLED S. P. HOLD-UP IN SISKIYOUS

but the baseball game story still held the No. 1 place
on the page—the far right column. The train holdup
story took spot No. 2 on the left column with a headline

TRAIN CREW ON NO. 13 ARE KILLED

followed immediately with the typical lengthy sub-head
of the era

    Engineer, Fireman, Brakeman
    and Mail Clerk Killed When
    Mail Car On Train 13 Blown
    Up in Tunnel By Bandits——
    Train Left Medford at 10:30
    A. M. This Morning.

  The story promptly identified the members of the
train's crew who had been murdered but said "a mail
clerk name unknown" had also been killed. While most
stories about this event merely talk about the deaths
of the railroadmen, many leave out the mail clerk apparently by reason the railroad accounts only for its
own. Mail clerks never worked for the railroads and
were not "manifested" as part of a train's crew. The
mail clerks worked for the United States Post Office
Department. The railroads maintained ready boards for
all the operations of the trains, and the Post Office
maintained it's own personnel schedules for manning the
RPOs. The railroaders and the mail men seldom had any
contact.

TRAIN CREW ON NO. 13 ARE KILLED

gineer, Fireman, Brakeman and Mail Clerk Killed When Mail Car On Train 13 Blown Up in Tunnel By Bandits— Train Left Medford at 10:30 A. M. This Morning.

Engineer S L. Bates of Dunsmuir, Calif., M Seng, fireman, of Dunsmuir. C. O. Johnson, brakeman. of Ashland, and a mail clerk name unknown, were kill d about one o'clock this afternoon in the Southern Pacific tunnel near Siskiyou when the mail car was dynamited and the train crew attacked by a band of armed bandits.

Thanks to quick action by the conductor of the train, further casualties were avoided, for the mail car took fire following the explosion and for a time the entire train was threatened. The conductor himself, according to report, ran the locomotive out of the tunnel and also brought all the cars out. The mail car was pulled out and side-tracked at White Point near Colestein where it burned to the ground.

It was nearly an hour after the holdup before word reached Ashland and although a posse was immediately organized the bandits got nearly a three hour start and their capture is considered doubt-

---

SISKIYOUS ARE FULL OF ARMED MEN ON HUNT

ASHLAND, Ore., Oc. 12.—The rough country on both sides of the Oregon-California line near here, armed with armed men today, all seeking some trace of the robbers who held up a southbound Southern Pacific passenger train yesterday in tunnel thirteen, killed three trainmen and a mail clerk and wrecked the

---

LOOKING FOR WOMAN IN BANDIT CASE

Authorities Looking for Woman Seen Near Siskiyou Tunnel at Time of Murder and Hold-Up—More Clues Unearthed But None of Much Importance.

The inevitable woman made her appearance in the Siskiyou tunnel train robbery and murder today and authorities, according to report, are looking for a lady garbed in a

---

BANDIT CLUE IS REPORTED AT ROSEBURG

ROSEBURG, Ore., Oct. 13.— Ford Jenkins has advised authorities here that four men in an automobile arrived at his garage here from the south late Thursday and departed early Friday. He said he found a can of pepper in their car and that the register in which he had entered their names disappeared at that time.

Clippings from the Medford *Mail Tribune*, Medford, Oregon.

Southern Pacific printed 2,000 "WANTED" posters (see page ii) that same day. Poster No. 3, in what would eventually number 23 editions numbering over 23,583,000 copies, was printed in the Medford newspaper office—5000 copies. Glossy snapshots of the men were hand-pasted on each poster.

Under Cover

The De Autremont boys must have been pretty tense on arrival at their hideout and probably didn't sleep much that night. They would imagine that it would not be long before search parties were send into the forest to look for them. They were surely correct with that thought for the sheriff was quickly mounting a posse and there were what some call "vigilante" groups of off-duty railroad men also combing the woods. Company B of the 186th Infantry, Oregon National Guard from Medford was mustered. Elements of this unit were sent to each end of Tunnel 13 to mount guard. As we understand today, the National Guard callup was for only about 24-hours. "I remember it was just overnight" recalled Chet Silliman in 1988. He was about 16 at the time and had enlisted "underage—I was 15 but they took me cause I looked older," he said. He packed a rifle, a .30 Springfield model 1903. "But we didn't have any bullets cause I guess the sergeant wouldn't trust us with any shells." Now in his eighties, he laughed about it but said he "felt dead serious at the time and come to think about I don't think we ever got paid for that duty"! His duty post was at the west end of the tunnel. He recalled that by the time he and the other Guardsmen got there—they had to walk through the damp tunnel—a railroad repair crew was already clearing up the mess and the corpses of the dead were "stretched out on a small flat car, one of those little work cars that is usually pulled behind a track-crew's handcar." He described the bullet holes in the bodies and said that engineer, Sidney Bates, still had his glasses on.

In the days that followed, airplanes were heard flying near tree tops apparently in search of the bandits. The three De Autremonts stayed under cover. They were well-provisioned and could stay there for a couple of weeks if need be.

Time wore on the brothers as their quarters were very close and none dared venture far from the hideout. As supplies were running out, it was decided Ray would try to get back to town. He made his way back to the west end of Tunnel No. 13, where all the deaths had occurred, to find the area cleaned and

The De Autremont brothers used this cabin high in the Siskiyou mountains before the holdup. Signs on each boarded up window read, "No Trespassing On This Land." (Below) Although there were hundreds of men in sheriff's posses, vigalante groups and even the National Guard searching the forests for the murder-bandits, what chance of finding them did they have considering the expanse of heavy trees and dense underbrush and almost no roads?

little trace of the event. He hopped a slow-moving
train as the train entered the tunnel then jumped
off as the train came into the Medford yard.

On seeing a copy of the Medford paper with his
picture and that of Roy on the front page, Ray was
stunned. He probably felt as though he could be
picked up by anyone any minute so he slipped out of
town spying Southern Pacific posters on walls, on
telephone poles—just about everywhere—hawking a
$14,400 for them alive or dead. He took a temporary
job picking fruit in a local orchard somewhere in the
area in the triangle of Medford, Central Point and
Jacksonville. When Ray had earned a little money,
he bought foods of a type he could carry easily and
still hop a freight train with free hands back up
the mountain. When he reached the hideout well after
dark, he told his brothers, who were quick to make a
meal on the newly acquired foods, of the rewards and
all the "WANTED" posters he had seen. Ray also told
of the many dozens of men who were searching the
forest looking for them.

They decided to break camp. They had bedrolls,
some food, one pistol and the shotgun. It was October
29th—eighteen days after the murders and botched
train holdup when the De Autremonts left. They had
been gone just a short time when it started to snow.
They saw deer, shot at them but missed. They came
upon an isolated cabin in which they found some food.
They continued on, but with strength running out due
to lack of food, started to discard their belongings
including their bedrolls. They were now probably
over the Oregon line and in California. They were
bone-weary. They broke in to logging camp kitchens
at night and took food. They were chilled to the
bone as they had no winter clothing. At night they
cautiously built fires, but were constantly aware
they might be spotted. Several times men saw them,
including the railroad dicks (detectives) near Hilt.
Each time the brothers paid no heed to calls to them,
and wandered off just like any hobo might do. It was
only a few days later when it was decided that to try
to continue together was foolhardy and they should
split up.

It was a cold November day, along the banks of the
Klamath River, when the unbathed men with dirty
clothing bid each other goodbye.

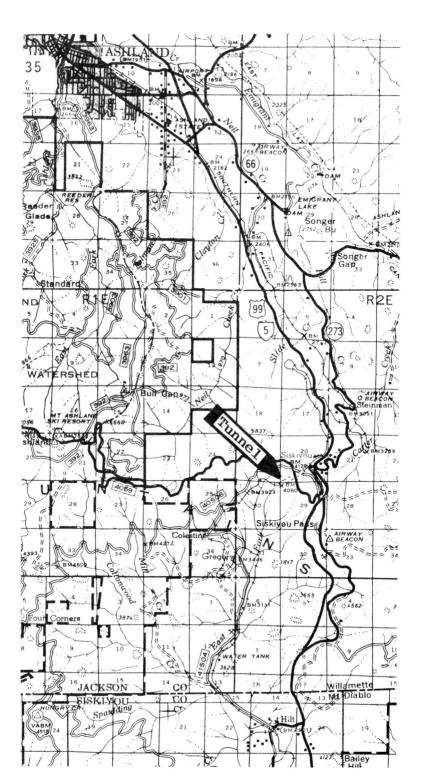

Roy De Autremont and two views of Ray De Autremont.
These snapshots were used on "WANTED" posters.

Roy and Ray

Roy and Ray kept fairly good communication between them and though each picked up odd jobs here
and there, eventually were reunited in Detroit during
December 1924.

But the heat was on in Michigan and "WANTED"
posters seemed to be everywhere. They had close
calls. They did not hear from Hugh. They took
casual employment when and where ever they could
find it, always being mindful of being "looked" at.

Roy and Ray decided to change their appearances.
They bleached their hair and Roy grew a "cookie-
duster" (mustache). To try to establish new identi-
ties they also decided they'd claim Arkansas as their
home residence. Next, they assumed the name
"Goodwin." Roy became "Clarence" and Ray took
"Elmer."

In the spring of 1925 they found work in the timber
business near Ironton, Lawrence County, Ohio. They
set up housekeeping in a small cabin in the woods.

One of the timber cruisers in the neighborhood had
a place nearby and invited the boys to dinner. James
Sprouse was his name. He had a large family—7
daughters and 5 sons. He and the "Goodwin" brothers
got along well. Ray was a frequent visitor to the
Sprouse place and he and 16-year old Hazel took a
special liking for each other. In just a few months

they slipped over the line into Kentucky where they were married. It was now August 1925. On June 15th little Jackie Hugh was born.

About six months later Roy found a job in coal mining at the Wheeling Steel Corporation's mine at Steubenville. A couple of months later Ray joined Roy and the two worked in the same place. About this period, it came to their attention that "WANTED" posters took on a different look. Across Hugh's portrait was heavy black type stating that Hugh had been captured but the other two men were still at large.

There was some talk about beating it to Mexico as the boys were fairly fluent in Spanish, but money shortage held up this plan. Instead of getting out of town immediately, they continued to work needing more money for the trip. But Roy was recognized and caught while he was on the job. Ray's capture followed almost immediately. The date was June 8, 1927.

The arrests had been made possible by one Albert Collingsworth, who had read about the train holdup and murders in far away Oregon years earlier and had actually worked with the "Goodwin" boys about one year earlier. As Collingsworth was bed-ridden due to an accident, he made contact with Emma Maynard who operated as the Maynard Detective Agency. The two cut a deal that each would share the reward. Mrs. Maynard notified the Department of Justice in Columbus, and the rest is history. There had been a number of actors in the actual apprehension—six men. Each got $100 for his services but the rest of the money went to Collingsworth and Maynard, each getting $4,150.00. In 1927 that was a lot of money!

Hugh De Autremont.
Photo from "WANTED" poster.

Hugh

Hugh De Autremont, 19, took the name James C.
Price. He was hungry, dirty, and tired out from the
ordeal in the woods following the bungled robbery
attempt. He rode the rods of freight trains to
southern California then to Texas and to Arkansas.
He traveled to the east coast then to Louisiana,
always on the move except for a few days work here
and there to keep alive. In the spring of 1924 he
found himself in Chicago, hungry as usual. Chicago
seemed like a tough town and he sensed danger at
every turn. One day while walking the streets, he
passed an army recruiting office with its brightly
colored posters describing life in the army and the
glories of foreign service. If he joined the army,
he reasoned, he would get three meals a day, a bed
and clothing. He'd have a roof over his head and
maybe, just maybe, he wouldn't have to run any more.
He joined on April 22, 1924. He told the officers
he was born in Houston, Texas, and he had no rela-
tives. His first station was Fort Sheridan, Illinois
but he was soon sent to Fort Slocum in New York to
await transfer by ship to the Presidio of San Francisco by way of the Panama Canal. At the Presidio
he was earmarked for trans-shipment to service in
the Philippines. He boarded ship as a "casual,"
unassigned except for transportation. On arrival
in Manila, he was put in B Company, 31st Infantry.
Hugh, that is "James Price," was careful with his
contacts, did his duty and stayed out of trouble.
He lived the good life within the confines of army
duty. In peacetime, life in a garrison was often
sought by the down-and-out for the same reason Hugh
signed up; meals, a bed, clothing, and a roof over
his head and a few dollars a month "pay."
It was a couple of years later when Sergeant
Reynolds, from B Company, arrived at Angel Island
embarkation center in San Francisco Bay for temporary
duty pending discharge. On July 2, he spotted a
"WANTED" poster on which he recognized the photograph
of one of his soldiers, Private James C. Price. The
description was identical.
At the earliest opportunity, Sgt. Reynolds took
the army ferry from Angel Island to the mainland,

Sergeant Thomas Reynolds, U.S. Army, recognized photograph of Hugh De Autremont on "WANTED" poster in California as a man in the sergeant's former outfit in the Philippine Islands. With Hugh's identification, one thing lead to another and all three brothers were caught.

then took a street car to Southern Pacific's headquarters. This is when he talked with the SP Agent for San Francisco, Mr. William H. Stone. Stone was flabbergasted at what the army sergeant told him so the two went immediately to the main post office to see the Postal Inspector in Charge.

Available records on Private Price were checked. These were proved sketchy to the point of making investigators curious. On November 17, 1926, Inspector Fred Smith was directed to seek the assistance of the Army and if necessary to proceed to Manila to investigate Private Price to see if indeed he was Hugh De Autremont.

There were no airplanes flying transpacific routes in those days thus travel time was extended for a trip nearly half way around the world. Postal Inspector Smith did not get to the Philippines for a long time. When he did, the Army knew he was coming (having been advised by cablegram) so cooperation was already waiting. Hugh De Autremont, alias Private James C. Price, was picked up on the 11th of February 1927. He was returned to Angel Island, California on the U.S. Army Transport *Thomas*.* Once landed, he was

---

* It occurs that Chester "Chet" Silliman, the young National Guardsman who had pulled guard duty at the tunnel within hours of the train holdup, had transferred to the Regular Army. He was sent to duty in the Philippines in 1927 also aboard *Thomas*. Although he had never met Hugh De Autremont, alias James C. Price, he quickly heard of Hugh's capture by the usual army word-of-mouth rumors. Hugh was indeed in the 31st Infantry, B Company, and had been stationed in Cuartel de España, the old walled city within Manila. Silliman became a mail clerk in I Company at Estada Mayor.

Chester Silliman was a private in B Company, 186th Infantry of the Oregon National Guard when his outfit was mustered to stand guard with Springfield 1903 .30 caliber rifles on the night of the murders and train holdup. He told the authors "we were so young, I was 16, that the officers wouldn't give us any bullets." He and the other guards saw no suspicious people during their duty. He missed Hugh then, and again in the Philippines in 1927 when Silliman arrived and Hugh De Autremont departed on the same ship.

whisked to the barracks on Alcatraz as a prisoner.
Although Hugh's mother was brought in from New Mexico in an effort by authorities to trick Hugh into confession, Hugh was able to signal his mother not to talk thus postal and railroad officers learned nothing. About a week later, Hugh was turned over to Sheriff Ralph Jennings of Jackson County Oregon for return to Jacksonville to stand trial.

Pair of creosote-covered overalls
abandoned in woods, along with the
Dupont blasting device as well as a
knapsack which had been intended
to carry loot. These, and other
items of evidence quickly identified the culprits as the three De
Autremont brothers, Ray, Roy and
Hugh.

(Inset) Creosoted shoe-covers
were part of the plot to throw
off bloodhounds.

All the "threads" of evidence were studied by criminologist Edward O. Heinrich of Oakland California. His precision clearly marked the De Autremont brothers as the sure targets for capture.

RECEIPT FOR REGISTERED ARTICLE

Registered at the Post Office Indicated in Postmark

No. _____

Class postage _____

Complete record of registered mail is kept at the post office, but the sender should write the name of the addressee on back hereof as an identification. Preserve and submit this receipt in case of inquiry.

POSTMASTER,

Form 3806.   Per_____

Postmark clearly showing date and office.

Receipt for Registered mail was first overlooked, then found in bottom of the center pocket of the bib-overalls. This receipt was quickly traced to the De Autremonts.

Hugh Stands Trial

As can be seen, Hugh's capture in the Philippine Islands, and the sunsequent re-release of the "WANTED" posters showing he had been caught, and the appearance of these new posters in Ohio, played a part in the seizure of Ray and Roy. Further, we earlier mentioned, hundreds of feature writing reporters grasped the story of the murders and did articles for their local papers. One of these articles had led to Ray and Roy. But all this took a lot of time—years in fact. But it was all coming together.

On Monday, May 2, 1927, Hugh De Autremont marched into the Jackson County Court House in the company of his jailers and attorneys. He went up the spiral stairs to the second floor court room and went directly to his place at the defense table. His mother was in the room. The next three days passed slowly and painfully as the court clerk called over 200 citizens among whom only twelve could serve as jurors.

These jurors were

Bush, B. M.	Willow Springs
Clemens, James E.	Medford
Davis, C. W.	Medford
Dunham, S. W.	Medford
Earhart, Frank	Medford
Fredenburg, Fred	Medford
Heberling, S. E.	Central Point
Judy, E. N.	Griffin Creek
Kime, Nick W.	Medford
Piche, Albert	Medford
Ward, A. W.	Eagle Point
Wiley, F. W.	Central Point

The trial was considered so important that the jurors were to be sequestered in a hotel and were directed by the court to have no communication with anyone, even among themselves about the trial except

44

George M. Roberts was in charge of
prosecution during the trial.

Daniel O'Connell, Chief Special
Agent for Southern Pacific Company.

Judge C. M. Thomas sentenced the De Autremont brothers to life in the Oregon State Penitentiary.

when in session. The trial began May 5th. C. M. Thomas, judge of the circuit court was on the bench. George M. Roberts and George Neuner prosecuted.

John Collier acted for the defense.

Prosecution was a two-pronged spear. There was the matter of the murders normally a county affair. Then the blowing up of the Railway Post Office car and murder of a federal employee, Dougherty, the mail clerk on the train, brought federal prosecution. The case was very involved.

Southern Pacific sent its chief special agent Dan O'Connell and Frank Ramirez, an SP investigator. The County had former Coroner, a Dr. Holt, testify he, just a couple weeks earlier, dug up the body of brakeman Johnson for re-examination and to remove the slugs from the corpse that had killed him. The prosecutors had all the trappings from the mountain cabin the De Autremonts had used prior to the crime including scraps from a slab of bacon from a pan on

Desk behind which Judge Thomas presided. This desk is preserved at the Jacksonville Museum of the Southern Oregon Historical Society. The museum was the county courthouse at the time of the trial.

the stove. Searchers had easily found the empty cartridges from the gun shots at the tunnel. They had them for the trial. In planning the crime, the boys had soaked gunny-sacks in creosote to wear over their shoes to fool tracking dogs. The smelly sacks turned up as evidence at the trial. Bib-overalls, which had been discarded, appeared as evidence as did the hand gun Roy had dropped on the tracks of the east end of the tunnel when he was scrambling to climb on the train. The boys had abandoned their knapsacks, in which they intended to carry loot, when they scurried away from the tunnel. These were there. And the Dupont dynamite detonator was in the center of the evidence table. The display was intended to be awesome. It was.

Hugh's trial went according to the book. There were presentations and examinations. Cross-examinations and hassels between attorneys were common. Much of the argument was tiresome and as a newspaper article pointed out, a juror loudly chewed gum

C. Riddiford, Postal Inspector in Charge at Spokane, Washington, and Tennyson Jefferson, Postal Inspector also from Spokane were prepared to present the case for the United States Post Office Department in the trial of Hugh De Autremont.

through it all. Another juror cracked and ate peanuts continuously. All this drama came to an abrupt end when S. W. Dunham, one of the jurors, became ill and died a few days later. Judge C. M. Thomas was forced to declare a mistrial. The jury was dismissed and Hugh De Autremont was returned to his cell in the jail next door to the court house.

Hugh's second trial began on June 6 with the selection of a new jury. Luckily for all, this enpaneling did not take so much time. The new jury

RECOMPENSA!
$14,400.00
CUATRO HOMBRES MUERTOS

Asalto Armado En El Tren Del Sureste (Meridional) Del Pacifico No. 13 Primera Seccion En Siskiyou, El Dia 11 De Octubre, De 1923.

Una recompensa de $2,500—sera pagada por la Compañia del Ferrocarril del Sureste del Pacifico, una de $300 —por la AMERICAN RAILWAY EXPRESS COMPANY (Compañia Americana del Ferrocarril Expreso), y otra que no excedera la suma de $2,000—por los Estados Unidos, por el arresto o prisión, declaraciones y condenación de cada una de las personas complicadas en aquel asalto del ferrocarril.

Son, por lo menos, tres personas las complicadas en aquel crimen.

Las fotografias y descripciones indicadas mas abajo corresponden a los tres hermanos que se cree estan en conexión con el referido asalto y que deben ser arrestadas tan pronto como se les vea, conservandoseles incomunicados.

DESCRIPCIONES

No. 1. Roy DeAutremont—Edad: 23 años. Peso; 135 a 140 libras; Pelo; ligeramente castaño; Altura: 5 pies y 8 pulgadas. Tez; medianamente clara; Ojos; Pequeños y algo obscuros; usa lentes en la nariz para leer, los ojos parecen granulados y blancos; la cara es ancha; cuello corto, nariz larga y de prominentes aberturas. Semblante de cara llana. Notiene marcas. Cabeza redonda.

No. 2. Ray DeAutremont—Edad: 23 años. Altura: 5 pies y 6 pulgadas; peso: 135 a 140 libras; calló a ley; medianamente clara, pelo; medianamente claro castaño; cara ancha; prominentes aberturas en la nariz; cuello corto; semblante llano; ojos pequeños ligeramente obscuros. Diente del ado derecho del ojo artificado con oro. Clasificación de la impresión.

11 1MM 11
20 0II 11

Fué condenado a un año de reclusión en Monroe, Washington. Estuvo en Casa de Corrección en Noviembre 17 de 1912. I. W. W. Reformista. Usa antiojos para leer.

No. 3. Hugh DeAutremont. Edad: 19 años; pero parece de mayor edad. Altura: 5 pies y 7 pulgadas; peso: 135 libras; cara limpia; ojos azules serio ligeramente romana; pelo; algo claro, arenoso y crespo, blanqueado por el sol; suavemente afeitado.

Usa un corto arrigo impermeable, también tenia mackinaw, pero no se sabe de qué color.

Los hombres arriba señalados y descritos son hermanos gemelos (Mellizos). Es bastante difícil para aquellas que no estan familiarizadas con ellos a distinguirlos y notar la diferencia entre ellos, separadamente.

El diferente aspecto consiste en que Ray, probablemente pesa tres o cuatro libras mas y que él es un poquito mas alto que Roy. También es confidido. Ray es mas rollizo. Hay es conservador y esta dispuesto a bromear mientras que Roy, notase, es mas inclinado a estar tranquilo; no están arrogante ni presumido en sus vestidos. Ambos han aprendido el oficio de barberos y han trabajado en los bosques, y en el trabajo de madera, y por consiguiente es presumir que se buscarán algun otro bien vestidos, tienen ahora la ropa ordinaria de los obreros llamados (troqueros) (loggers) que se ocupan de los troncos de los arboles.

Todos los tres individuos son loggers (tronqueros) obreros que trabajan en los bosques, y probablemente pueden ser hallados en los campos de madera, en donde se les ocupa como: Choker-Setter, Hook-tenders, o bien como: Whistle punks. (diferentes empleos en—los campos de madera).

Ellos han manifestado tener la intención de hacer un largo viaje de mar y por consiguiente conviene vigilar y averiguar su paradero a bordo de los vapores anclados en los puertos por que han de pretender embarcarse.

Hablan correctamente el español y han de tratar de cruzar la frontera méxicana. Anteriormente vivian en Lakewood, New México.

Las fotografias de Roy y de Hugh fueron sacadas hace un año poco mas ó menos; y la de Ray, en el año 1920.

Dirijanse los datos y demas informaciones telegráficamente a D. O'Connell, Jefe-Agente Especial del Ferrocarril Sudeste Pacifico (SOUTHERN PACIFIC RAILROAD COMPANY), Ashland, Oregon; C. E. Terrill, Sheriff, Jackson County, Jacksonville, Oregon—ó también a C. Riddiford, Post Office Inspector in Charge, Spokane, Washington.

Los Directores de las Oficinas de Correo pondran los respectivos avisos las publicaran y los distribuiran entre los Conductores Rurales de Caminos e igualmente cuidarande que los Agentes o Alguaciles tengan a su disposición estas circulares.

C. RIDDIFORD,
Inspector Encargado de la Oficina
de Correo, Spokane, Washington.

D. O'CONNELL,
Jefe-Agente Especial del Ferrocarril (Southern Pacific R. R. Co.), Ashland, Oregon.

Case No. 57883-D

(Spanish)

No. 6   Printed November 13, 1923.   Ten thousand copies, $20.00.

was made up of different people. Gone was the gum-
chewer and the peanut cracker.

Daniels, R. S.	Medford
Darby, Wm. F.	Ashland
Dutton, Fred B.	Medford
Farlow, Thos.	Lake Creek
Frame, Henry W.	Phoenix
Hittle, W. W.	Gold Hill
Kerney, M. J.	Central Point
Marin, Paul W.	Central Point
Miller, Frank	Ashland
Norcross, L. O.	Ashland
Weaver, Earl W.	Central Point
Wideman, R. A.	Eagle Point

George Roberts, who prosecuted this second trial
started from scratch on June 10th. For the defense,
Fred Smith was direct and to the point. Where
Attorney Roberts had taken much more than an hour
with a recitation of all of the events up to the
death of juror Dunham, Smith's speech was a bare five
minutes. It was imperative that the prosecutor con-
vince the jury that Hugh had been at the scene.
Defense attorney Smith believed the State could not
prove its case and said so.

One of the witnesses for the prosecution was train
No. 13's baggageman Hugh Haffey who had taken the
peek when the train was stopped in the tunnel, then
was knocked unconscious by the blast of dynamite.
But testimony of Dr. Ernest O. Heinrich, a criminologist whose precise study of evidence quickly pointed
fingers not only at Hugh but also Roy and Ray who
had, in the meantime, been picked up in Ohio and were
even then on the way to Jacksonville under guard of
Sheriff Ralph Jennings.

A receipt for Registered Mail was found in the
small pocket in the bib overalls and was easily
traced. It had covered a letter from Roy, containing
a life insurance policy, to another brother, Verne.
That receipt, claim many, proved the association of
the De Autremonts, the overalls, and the train holdup
as the overalls were found at the site.

How could a defense attorney overturn such
evidence?

Hugh's trial came to an end when the judge ordered
the jurors to their deliberating room and to return
with two decisions. The first, either guilty or not
guilty. The second, if guilty, the penalty. The
jury did not take very long for in only an hour and
24 minutes later they filed back into the courtroom.
The foreman announced Hugh was guilty of first degree

$15,900.00 REWARD
IN GOLD
Train Hold-up and Murder

Hugh DeAutremont has been Arrested.
Ray ... At Large.

MAIL CAR AFTER HOLDUP.
Where the postal clerk was cremated.

Case No. 57883-D

$15,900.00 Reward in Gold!

murder. The jury recommended life imprisonment.

Meanwhile in the little jailhouse, Roy and Ray were hearing what was going on in the Court House next door. Although the twins had stated they were not guilty, after many hours of discussions, which included the judge, train officials, Post Office Department people and lawyers, all agreed that the circumstantial evidence against them would probably never bring a death penalty thus it was finally decided in exchange of pleadings of guilty and full confessions, an understanding was made that the twins would also be sentenced to life in the Oregon State Penitentiary. (The twins never went to trial.)

This was carried out.

A week later (June 27, 1927) the three brothers:

Hugh De Autremont   Ore. S.P. 9902
Ray De Autremont   Ore. S.P. 9903
Roy De Autremont   Ore. S.P. 9904

took up life at the state Penitentiary in Salem with work assignments in the prison's lime works.

The Oregon State Penitentiary was the end of the trail for all three De Autremont brothers. Folklore tells that every time a train passed the penitentiary, it would sound its whistle and ring its bell as a reminder to the inmate-De Autremonts of their crime.

The De Autremont twins assumed jaunty attitudes, posed for cameras, sang songs in jail as distraction to law officers and to the enjoyment of the Steubenville, Ohio folks who flocked to the jail to see these "desperados."

DE AUTREMONTS ARRESTED

OFFICE OF CHIEF INSPECTOR,
Washington, June 13, 1927.

All three of the fugitive De Autremont brothers, wanted in Oregon for mail-train holdup and murder, have been apprehended by the Post Office Department and are awaiting trial. Hugh De Autremont was arrested at Manila, P. I., February 11, 1927, and Roy and Ray De Autremont were arrested at Steubenville, Ohio, on June 9, 1927.

Postmasters are requested to clip this notice from the BULLETIN and paste it securely to the bottom of the De Autremont circular posted in their offices. The circulars with the notice affixed should then remain posted for 30 days, after which they may be taken down. Please see to it that this is done. If sufficient copies of the BULLETIN notice are not available, please write or print with a rubber stamp across each of the remaining circulars these words in large letters:

CANCELED

ALL THREE OF THESE MEN ARE UNDER ARREST.
CHIEF INSPECTOR.

Postmasters will please bring this notice to the attention of local peace officers and give it otherwise the widest circulation possible without expense to the department.

I sincerely thank all for the thoroughly good work done for us in this case.

GRANT B. MILLER,
Chief Inspector.

Jackson County Deputy Sheriff Lewis
Jennings escorts Roy De Autremont
into Court House for trial.

De Autremont twins being escorted by Jackson County Deputy
Sheriff Lewis Jennings (with cap) at door of jail, from the
jail to the Court House next door. (Right) Jackson County
Court House of 1927 is now the Jacksonville Museum of the
Southern Oregon Historical Society. The De Autremont trial
was the last major trial held here before county seat moved
to Medford.

Albert Collingsworth recognized a picture of the twins,
Ray and Roy, in a newspaper feature story as the young
men known to him as the Goodwin brothers in Ohio. Mr.
Collingsworth reported his discovery to Mrs. Emma L.
Maynard, who operated as the Maynard Dective Agency.
She passed the information along to government agents.
She and Collingsworth each received $4,140 of reward
money.

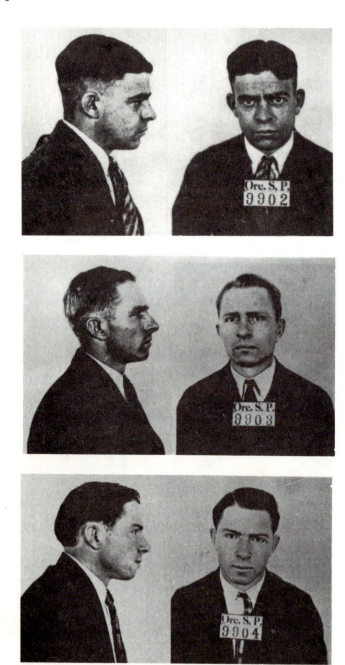

Hugh De Autremont
Oregon State Penitentiary No. 9902

Received from Jackson County June 25, 1927
CRIME: Murder, First Degree, Life
Age: 23 in 1927
Complexion: Light
Eyes: Blue
Hair: Light Brown   [Observe: Height missing]
Weight: 125 lbs
Build: Small
Native Arkansas. French-German descent.
Little Finger left hand curved inward; round scar back of
right hand; large oval scar inside right wrist; round scar
right side back head; two round scars on right groin.

Ray De Autremont
Oregon State Penitentiary No. 9903
Received from Jacksin County June 24, 1927
CRIME: Murder, First Degree, Life
Age: 27 in 1927
Complexion: Medium
Eyes: Light Reddish Brown
Weight: 123 lbs
Height: 5 feet 6 inches
Build: Slight   [Observe: Hair color missing]
Native Arkansas. French-German descent.
Round blotch scar about 1/2 size of dime on right cheek; pit
scar under left jaw; two boil scars back of neck; upper front
tooth missing; left great toe nail deformed.

Roy De Autremont
Oregon State Penitentiary No. 9904
Received from Jackson County June 24, 1927
CRIME: Murder, First Degree, Life
Age 27 in 1927
Complexion: Medium
Eyes: Light Redding Brown
Hair: Light brown
Weight: 127 lbs
Height: 5 feet 5 inches
Build: Slight
Native Arkansas. French-German descent.
Small mole on right cheek; brown scar on outside calf right leg;
round boil scar on right buttock; six round boil scars on left
leg above knee.

A Wife and Babies

As earlier related, Ray, under the name of Elmer
Goodwin, had married Hazel Sprouse while Ray was a
fugitive. Their first child, Jackie Hugh, was born
in June 1926. At the time of Ray's capture, the baby
was about one year old and Hazel was pregnant with
a second son. Her second baby was born in February
1928. Despite pressures from many sides, she announced the boy would be named for his father, Ray.

There seems no doubt that Ray and Hazel were deep-
ly in love. She wrote to Ray in the Oregon Penitentiary and he wrote back, regularly. Her parents wanted
her to forget him and to start life anew, even with
two babies.

Before the twins left for jail then trial in Oregon,
they had given all their money to Hazel. Shortly
after Roy and Ray entered the penitentiary, Hazel and
Jackie Hugh boarded a chair car for the long restless
train trip to Eugene, Oregon. The De Autremont's
father, Paul lived there. He was not very willing to
take his daughter-in-law and baby to see Ray in Salem,
nevertheless he was very happy to see the young girl
Ray had married and had always said only kind words
about. Paul De Autremont was proud to have a grand-

son, but he was worried about the future of little
Jackie Hugh and the yet unborn baby. He urged Hazel
to return to Ohio and forget her episode in life with
his son. But Hazel was lovingly defiant. She in-
sisted on visiting the three boys in prison thus,
about a week later, her father-in-law took her and
the child to see the brothers.

In the state penitentiary she was welcomed by all
three brothers but especially Ray, her husband and the
father of her child. It was during the visit she told
Ray she was "expecting" again. Ray said he would
send whatever money he earned as a worker in the
prison to her—about fifteen dollars a month. Hazel
stayed in Oregon at the De Autremont home in Eugene
until late fall then with money sent by her father,
took the train back to Ohio.

The strain of being alone with her babies and
without her husband was stressful on Hazel who tried
for years to keep her chin up with the hope that Ray's
confinement might be reduced. But this never happened.
Ray had urged her to file for divorce but she refused
for nearly twenty-five years grasping at the hope that
all this bad dream would resolve. In the meantime
her boys grew. Jack, as an adult, entered industry in
Ohio. Ray fought in the "police action" in Korea. On
his discharge, he was unable to adjust to civilian ways
and took his own life. Hazel remarried.

Years of Confinement and the End

The boys' mother, Belle De Autremont, had made her
home in Lakewood, New Mexico where she operated a small
store. She sold out and moved to Salem to be near her
boys. In Salem she ran a rooming house.

Hugh De Autremont, the youngest, became interested
in writing and took some courses through the facilities
of the University of Oregon. He became quite proficient
and apparently started the prison newspaper *The Shadows*.
In addition to writing skills be learned to operate a
Linotype typesetting machine. His thoughts, like the
thoughts of most prisoners, was "when would I get out
of this place"?

He was often interviewed by prison officials and
doctors who reported Hugh should do well in civilian
life, but these reports never recommended he be paroled. There were charges held by the Jackson County
Sheriff for immediate re-arrest if any of the three
were ever released. Railroad as well as postal office
people firmly believed the men should all spend their

lives behind bars as originally sentenced in 1927. In time opposition to parole lessened as old timers died or mellowed. Eventally, by legal maneuvering, and help from kind people, Hugh was paroled from the Oregon State Penitentiary on January 9, 1959. He was 55. He had served more than thirty-one years.

Hugh moved to San Francisco, under the control of the parole system of the State of California, in accordance with an agreement reached with Oregon authorities before his release. He obtained a job with one of the city newspapers as a Linotype operator. Regretably, within about a week, Hugh became ill and was hospitalized. Early in March he was diagnosed as having incurable cancer. He died in the hospital on March 30. He had been a free man just 81 days.

*　　　　*　　　　*

Roy DeAutremont seemed to get off to a pretty good start with life in confinement but over the years grew resentful. The two, Roy and Ray, as twins, had been granted cell-mate privilege from the start but now they no longer could get along. Roy seemed at odds with just about everything and everyone. He was adjudicated as mentally incompetent and transferred to the Oregon State Hospital for the Insane. There, he was sent to surgery for a prefrontal lobotomy which caused him to calm down. It was later claimed his hobbies included playing pool and drinking soda pop. Roy died in a nursing home in 1983.

*　　　　*　　　　*

Ray DeAutremont was granted a parole on October 26, 1961 using some of the legal format that had been applied to Hugh's parole. He had been jailed for nearly thirty-four years. Ray obtained a job on the custodial staff at the University of Oregon. He was 61. While in the penitentiary Ray had kept pretty much to himself and did a lot of reading. In time he learned French and Spanish and taught these languages to beginning language students in the penitentiary. Ray also learned to paint. His artistry became good enough that some of his work was sold in the gift shop. Ray had always wanted to be a free man and said what he and his brothers did was a stupid senseless thing. In 1972 then Governor Tom McCall announced,

> We should base our corrections program on reform rather than punishment...[De Autremont's] fine record of eleven years on parole [after nearly 34 years] incarcaration...then all the facts being brought to me [about] how [Ray De Autremont] could contribute to society...I [am] proud and happy to have the opportunity to do it.

With the stroke of his pen, the governor commuted Ray's two consecutive life terms. Ray was a free man.

Has Ray De Autremont ever returned to the scene of his crime? Portland television station KGW filmed a documentary in 1973. The sixty-minute program was broadcast in Portland and relayed by way of some community cable syetems. On December 10, KMED-TV replayed the program in Medford. The local staff added another thirty minutes to the presentation. Although many of his accusers were now dead, move away, or had forgiving minds, there were still quite a number in the

Rogue Valley (KMED-TV's main broadcast area) who were grossly provoked at the station for re-opening the old wound. And they said so in very direct terms to the station manager.

On September 6, 1973, Jack Pement, a Staff Writer for the *Oregon Journal* brought Ray De Autremont to Siskiyou for pictures to be included in a twelve-part serial Pement was preparing for his paper. Al Moner was the Staff Photographer. Bert Webber, as *Oregon Journal* "stringer" in the area, had worked with Pement on some of the plans but as Pement was under agreement with a publicity agent of De Autremont's, Webber stayed away on the day of the visit to the tunnel.

After the television programs and the newspaper feature appeared, Ray was often asked about the 1923 crime and gladly accepted requests for his autograph. But insofar as some old timers in the Ashland area were concerned, he was still considered a "ruthless killer who robbed [men of their lives], homes of husbands and fathers, leaving widows to shift for themselves."*

Ray De Autremont died in 1984.
All three brothers share a single headstone in Salem's Bellcrest Memorial Park.

* Quoted from interview of authors with Blanche Doughtery Rinebarger, whose husband was the murdered mail clerk on duty on Train No. 13, October 11, 1923.

We Leftovers

Mrs. Blanche Rinebarger told us, on being interviewed in 1974, she had never been asked in the last fifty years how the loss of her husband had interrupted their lives and that of their 4-year-old son, Raymond. "All of the attention went toward finding, then trying those murdering holdup men. My son and I, and the other wives, were merely leftovers-nobody seemed to care." She asked if she could tell her story:

We lived in Ashland and I was doing the fall housecleaning when Jack Edwards and his wife paid an unexpected visit soon after lunch. Jack was also a Railway Post Office clerk, The run that day (October 11, 1923) was Jack's, but he and Elvyn frquently swapped shifts. Elvyn was working extra to get several consecutive days off because he wanted to go hunting. He was a bird hunter. Mr. Edwards told me that the boiler on the engine had just blown up. He asked me if I wanted to go up the mountain with them. I told him that I was busy and didn't want to go, but Mrs. Edwards persisted. Although I didn't realize it at the time, this was the start of my being officially told that my husband was gone.

By the time we got there, the second section of the train had climbed the mountain and was stopped at Siskiyou on a siding. Trainmen were standing around. Most didn't know me because we weren't railroad people—we were government (postal). In the station one man recognized me and said right out that the mail clerk was dead. I couldn't believe it. I didn't go to the other end of the tunnel where the wreck was. I just stayed at Siskiyou for a little while. I don't really remember going back home but when we got there, my 4-year-old Raymond said, 'Mama, that man told you true!'

The funeral for Dougherty was in Ashland, then his remains were shipped to Reno, his home town, for burial.

In mid-morning, October, 11, 1923, Railway Postal Clerk Elvyn
Dougherty bid his wife and son good-bye and he was off to the
Ashland, Oregon Southern Pacific Railwoad station. He boarded
his mail car for his day's work.That morning was the last time
his wife and son ever saw him. He was killed in the dynamite
explosion that blew up the end of his mail car then the flash
fire that followed cremated his body.

As a clerk in a Railway Mail Service car, Elvyn Dougherty's
job was to receive and dispatch mail from way stations and
to sort mail while the train rolled along. Each RPO had
its own unique postmark. The postmark on Train No. 13,
the train known as "The San Francisco Express," read:
ASHLAND & SAN FRAN/ R.P.O./ TR 13/(date)

The Dougherty family: Elvyn, Raymond, Blanche with
their new Chevrolet touring car. Following her
husband's death, Blanche Dougherty sold the car as
she did not drive.

His widow and son did not go. Funerals for the three
murdered train men were in Medford, Oregon and in
Dunsmuir and Los Angeles, California.

> For weeks, every morning when I'd wake up,
> it was like a bad dream that would come and knock
> me in the head again. What had happened was hard
> for me to accept. My world was suddenly empty.
> Life was a drudge. Nobody knows the miles I walk-
> ed night after night. There were many worthless
> days but I had to keep busy.

Her husband had died without a will. She had bills.
The government allowed her $35 a month, survivor's
pension, plus all of $10 a month for Raymond. But it
took three months of paperwork before the first check
came. The widow Dougherty did a neighbor's washing and
ironing for pay and was hired part-time as a practical
nurse for an elderly friend. Since she didn't drive,
she sold their new Chevrolet touring car. Then she
sold all of her husband's camping and hunting gear.

Dougherty had a $3,000 policy from New York Life
Insurance Company. With $1,000 of this, his widow paid
off the second mortgage on their house, he having paid
off the first mortgage just four months before. She in-

Elvyn Dougherty was a bird hunter
and did very well at it, recalled
his wife. "He even cleaned them.
All I did was the cooking then the
eating."

vested the rest in Canadian bonds for her son. (When
Raymond was discharged from the United States Army in
1946 he realized the proceeds.)

Railway mail clerks expected a certain amount of
transfers. Raymond had been born in Alturas, Calif.,
Dougherty was from Reno, and had worked there. Ashland
was a "temporary" home. (Blanche Dougherty came from
England and had lived in Canada.) She said, "We had
few friends and I had no family to lean on. My son and
I seemed to be leftovers from a bad dream. I taught
Sunday School in Ashland's Methodist Church and this

Blanche Dougherty Rinagerber and author Bert Webber during interview. Mrs. Rinaberger pointed out that in the 1920's there was almost no support for crime victims. She received $35 each month as a survivor of a federal emoloyee and was allowed an extra $10 for her son. She did not like to recall those dark days in her life.

gave me what stability I could muster. Even so, it was nearly a year before I could look forward again.

In talking about it in 1974, she said it was not bringing up any new hurts because the hurt had always been there-just healed over.

> I didn't have any resentment or vengeance against my husband's killers because, as I look back on it now, I was too overwhelmed—grief-stricken. I told myself, 'They will find their own punishment!' Now, there seems to be no one left in 1974 but me to speak for the widows and children of the murdered men.

Engineer Sidney Bates and his wife had no children. They lived in Dunsmuir, California. Neighbors said after Sid's death that his wife just

68

'went to pieces.'

Marvin Seng lived with his wife and small daughter also in the railroad town of Dunsmuir. I have not seen or heard of them since the DeAutremont trial in 1927.

The murdered brakeman, Coyl Johnson, was married but had no children. His wife remarried but is now deceased.

I was disappointed to learn that Governor McCall freed Ray DeAutremont in November, 1972 . In my mind, Ray DeAutremont and his brothers will always be ruthless killers who robbed homes of husbands and fathers, leaving widows to shift for themselves.

Blanche Rinagerber
as a volunteer
seemstress at
Rogue Valley
Memorial Hospital
in Medford.

On December 7, 1925, Blanche Dougherty became the wife of Rollie Jay Rinabarger, a mechanic and welder with the Jackson County, Oregon, road department. In 1975 they celebrated their 50th anniversary. Her son, Raymond Dougherty, graduated from Oregon State College in 1941 and was with the U.S. Forest Service in San Francisco. The Rinagarger's daughter, Nancy, holds degrees from the University of Oregon and Southern Oregon Collete, and was a school teacher and librarian in Eagle Point, Oregon.

Blanche (Dougherty) Rinagarger joined the Red Cross as a volunteer nurse's aid during World War II while yet a homemaker and mother of a teenager. In 26 months she gave 3,700 hours of volunteer service. In November, 1944, the Community Hospital in Medford, where she had worked for the Red Cross (and the forerunner to the present Rogue Valley Medical Center) put her on the payroll as a nurse's aid. "My first check was $80, and that was the most I had earned at one time up until then," she declared.

When Oregon licensed practical nurses, she was awarded her LPN by waiver because of her training and proficiency. Following surgery in 1956, she retired "officially but not mentally," and in 1959 volunteered as a seamstress in the "mending room" at the hospital. In 1983 Blanche Rinagarger was 93, and as a member of the Rogue Valley Memorial Hospital Auxiliary, accumulated over 30,000 hours of volunteer sewing for which she was awarded a special volunteer service pin.

When she was 79 she lost her lower left leg to surgery but declared, "I'll walk again!"

She did. Without crutches.

She died February 21, 1984.

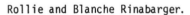

Rollie and Blanche Rinabarger.

Appendix A

The Experience of George DeMoss

George DeMoss was a resident of Medford. He was 27. His family lived in Selma (near Fresno) in California and he decided to visit them. He packed his suitcase then headed for the station to catch the southbound train, The San Francisco Express, Train No. 13. It was October 11, 1923.

Promptly at 10:30 A.M., the Conductor flagged the engineer to leave Medford station. DeMoss settled in his over-stuffed bench seat in the Pullman car—which was the last car on the train. He prepared himself for an uneventful trip even anticipating the near-sleepless night before him as almost no one slept well in a berth when compared to the bed at home. Maybe he had a copy of the new issue of *The Saturday Evening Post* to relax with.

Being an Express train, No. 13 puffed through the villages of Phoenix and Talent without stopping. It pulled into the Ashland station for passengers as well as for fresh drinking water. A few miles, after leaving Ashland, No. 13 puffed its way up the mountain through tight, grinding and squeeking turns and in some places those in the front cars might glance and see the last car alongside them, but at a lower level, such were the twists of the road.

The Express stopped at the summit, Siskiyou Station, to drop the extra engine needed to make the grade. Ashland is only 1,895 feet altitude and trains have always needed "helper" engines to reach the 4,130 feet altitude summit. In only minutes, the train was off again and in seconds entered a tunnel. It was not the only tunnel on this run. It was No. 13 of 16. These tunnels were relatively short, all less than one mile long thus lights in the cars were not turned on. But suddenly, although the train had been picking up speed, it ground to a sudden, jarring, screeching stop in the black of the tunnel.

DeMoss said that passengers sat in the dark in wonderment but he said there was no fear. Then came the explosion. The blast rocked the train, even back to the last car where he had his seat. George DeMoss said he didn't remember any yelling or screaming but there was almost instant confusion when the car became engulfed in smoke of a type, he said, that was different from usual "locomotive smoke." The air became stiffling all at once. People started to cough and had

trouble breathing. He and some others, made for the
rear door. They forced it open and then jumped to the
ground.

His car was inside the tunnel but not all that far
inside so he and the others ran to the exit (East
Portal). He said that within about a minute or so he
had to jump aside as another locomotive was about to
enter the tunnel behind the stalled train. DeMoss
recalled there were eight or so men on this second
engine as it passed him.

He acknowledged that by now some other passengers
had managed to get off various cars and were coughing
and stumbling their way out of the tunnel. The tunnel's mouth was now quite full of smoke and "it smel-
led pretty bad."

By now he had walked to the little station where he
recalled everyone there seemed very excited and all
were talking at the same time. He heard the word
"murders" and there was a lot of swearing among the
trainmen. Somebody said something about part of the
train had blown up.

The extra engine that had just entered the tunnel
was now pulling the train cars out, backwards onto a
switch track. DeMoss said all the cars were there
except the mail car and the locomotive. He didn't
know then what happened to separate them from the rest
of the train.

In the midst of this excitement along came the
second section of Train No. 13. It made the usual
stop to drop its "helper" locomotive. The crew on
that train did not know why the first section was on
the siding or what happened until told by the Siskiyou
station men.

DeMoss explained that the two Conductors, the one
from his train, and the Conductor from the second section, decided to place as many as possible of the passengers from the first train on the second section if
they wanted to continue their trips then. DeMoss was
in a hurry to get to Selma so he immediately held up
his hand and was given a place on the second train.

After he sat down he noticed his clothing was all
sooty but he couldn't do anything about it. He next
saw a few others get in the car who had been on the
earlier train. He remembered some of these people had
very dirty faces. Everybody was fairly quiet about the
event, he said, probably because none of them, including him, knew what happened until they read the next
day's newspaper.

George DeMoss related his story to the authors in
1973. He said his story had never been told to anyone
who would write about it before. Mr. DeMoss died in
1976.

Appendix B
Route to Tunnel No. 13

Readers are reminded that railroad rights-of-way are private property and are usually posted "No Trespassing." The author holds a permit to be on the railroad company property for the purpose of this project.

From Ashland, Oregon, proceed south on interstate freeway I-5 to Mt. Ashland offramp. This is near the summit of the Siskiyou mountains. Access to the east portal of Tunnel 13 is about one-quarter mile from the freeway and is an improved (gravel) narrow road on the right. Siskiyou Station is less than another quarter-mile. Watch out for trains! There is ample room for cars, light trucks and campers to turn around on north side of the access driveway—the area where the old turntable was located. No trace of the turntable today. About 100 yards south is the east portal to the tunnel. (Although the tunnel runs about north and south, in railroad language you are at the "east" portal.) One can see the tunnel to be a single tube thus the exit, 3,107.70 feet away can be viewed. It is never recommended one walk inside any railroad tunnel even though train schedules may have been consulted as "extra" trains may approach without notice. Should one enter the tunnel, notice even on hot summer days the temperature is always cool.

Siskiyou Station, MP 412 in October 1988

　　To visit "west" portal, proceed from the Mt. Ashland exit onto the road to Mt. Ashland ski area. Drive
2 miles on this road to a sign "Colestein Road'. on
left. Colstein Road is shown on Forest Service map as
Road 41S04 but the map, which see in this book, is a
1968 printing. Today this is Jackson County Road No.
993 but there are no signs so indicating on the road.
　　Turn to left and enter Colestein Road. The road is
narrow, gravel, steep and sharp turns. The road is
hardly recommended for large RVs but camper/pickup
units use this road frequently. Proceed 2.8 miles to
poorly seen unpaved (dirt) narrow road on left. This
road is not on any map known and will probably be
missed unless keen attention is given.to the scene as
well as to odometer. Take this road all of it's one-
quarter mile length—leads to railroad track at what
was once White Point siding. Observe the twin block
signals to right of front of vehicle at about "2 o'clock" position. These signals serve only as a checkpoint for your visit.   Turn left (north—up hill).
Proceed up-track along the track right-of-way but
stay away from the rails due to possible unexpected
trains. This area is fairly wide but watch for sharp
rocks.

74

(Above) The walk to West Portal from the convenient parking area is uphill and takes about 40 minutes. The return, all downhill, is about a 25 minute walk. (Lower) Area suggested for parking vehicles is opposite this old-style signal. There is no room to turn a trailer unit or RV here.

Drive .7 to end of drivable area which is across the track from a trackman's block indicator signal — see in picture. (This signal is no longer in service and is subject to removal at any time.) This signal serves as a checkpoint for your visit. You will note you have reached about as far as you can drive as the way has become narrow. Turn your vehicle around for easy departure and park here away from the rails. It is ill-advised to leave valuables in the vehicle. There seems to be space for about four vehicles to park but surely no RVs or cars with trailers can turn here. Authors used a Honda CIVIC for this trip.

Enjoy a drink of water or soft drink here before starting the up-track hike of about 1.5 miles to the tunnel.

Walk alongside the track—not between the rails as trains drip oil and throw grease. These lubricants are nearly impossible to clean off shoes. Be aware this soil on shoes inflicts damage to pants cuffs and may later be tracked into your vehicle.

Walking time to tunnel is about 40 minutes. The return walk is about 25 minutes. Be careful. There are no emergency phones and no residences in the area. (While we are not aware of any marajuana farming here, the practice seems common in southern Oregon thus visitors need to stay out of the woods and keep in plain sight of each other and near the tracks.)

This is railroad property with right to trespass revokable at any time without notice.

At the tunnel:

This tunnel, as earlier mentioned, is single tube thus the east portal can be seen in the distance. When the authors visited there, one could see the inscription on the wall when the gunnite finish was sprayed on the tunnel as a weather preservative.

About the only things to do at the west portal is to sit and rest, take some pictures, then walk back down-track to the vehicle.

One may leave the area by continuing down the road to some residences near where the road crosses the track. This is Colestein. There was once a large summer resort and mineral water bottling plant here as well as a post office (Apr. 8, 1892—Aug. 10, 1943) and there had been a post office at White Point (Aug. 8, 1883—Apr. 8, 1892). This road crosses into California and passes the site of the village of Hilt. This was a "company" town and was removed in the 1970s. Rejoin I-5 at a junction east of Hilt.

Appendix C

Siskiyou Subdivision
Southern Pacific Transportation Company
Gradients and Altitudes by Mile Posts
Ashland, Oregon — Hilt, California

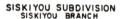

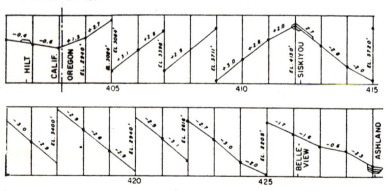

Appendix D

$15,900 REWARD

FOUR MEN MURDERED

Holdup Southern Pacific Co. Train 13, Siskiyou, Ore., Oct. 11, 1923

Record of "WANTED" circulars published

Circular Number	Date	Quantity	Cost ($)	Remarks
1	Oct 11 1923	2,000	75.00	Reward, $2,500 each person
2	Oct 13	10,000	100.00	
3	Oct 21	5,000	600.00	Reward $4,800 each person
4	Oct 24	30,500	200.00	Reward: $14,400 total. $2,500 from SP; $300 from American Railway Express; "not to exceed $2,000," United States.
5	Nov 13	40,000	60.00	
6	Nov 13	10,000	20.00	(Spanish)
7	Nov 30	4,000	8.00	(Spanish)
8	Jun 2, 1924	100,000	243.58	
9	Apr 10, 1926	2,500	50.00	Circular for Ray DeAutremont only includes finger prints. Sent to world wide finger print bureaus. Reward: $5,300 each man.
10	Apr 21	24,000	35.00	Reward: $15,900 total ($500 added by State of Oregon.) Sent to Masters of ships on the Atlantic and Pacific Oceans.
11	May 17,1926	1-Million	2,947.55	Reward: $15,900 (total) "in GOLD"
12	Jul 23	140,000	361.27	
13	Jul 23	260,000	670.90	
14	Dec-1926	20,000	207.31	(French)
15	Dec-1926	80,000	417.09	(Spanish)
16	Jan 27, 1927	100,000	298.00	
17	Feb-1927	60,000		(Special supplement to *Postal Bulletin*)
18	Apr-1927	10,000	128.21	(Dutch) Overprinted: Hugh caught.
19	Apr-1927	10,000	128.75	(German) Overprinted: Hugh caught.
20	Apr 11	500,000	2,129.55	Reward $10,600 ($5,300 each for Roy and Ray—Hugh caught.)
21	Apr-1927	20,000	207.84	(French)
22	Apr-1927	105,000	595.86	(Spanish)
23	Apr-1927	50,000	406.22	(Portugese)
23		2,583,000	9,911.06	

Appendix E

Memorials

**Mr. Johnson, the brakeman, is buried
in the I.O.O.F. (Eastwood) Cemetery
in Medford, Oregon.**

Mr. Seng, the fireman, is buried in
the cemetery in Dunsmuir, California.

Mr. Bates, the engineer.
Quoted from the *Dunsmuir News*, October 12, 1923:
Sidney Bates' body will be taken to Los Angeles
to be cremated. He was a member of the Blue
Lodge Royal Arch Chapter and Sciots.

Mr. Dougherty, the Railway Mail
Service's clerk, is believed to
be buried in Reno, Nevada.

**The three De Autremont brothers are
buried in Bellcrest Memorial Park
in Salem, Oregon.**

Bibliography

"Blanche Rinaberger, 93, Longtime Volunteer, Dies" in
    Medford *Mail Tribune*, Feb. 22, 1984
"Bloodhounds Leading Man Hunt in Hills for Railroad
    Bandits" in Medford *Mail Tribune*, Oct. 12, 1923
Chipman, Art. *Tunnel 13*. Pine Cone. (1977)
"D'Autremont Brothers, Train Robbery, Subject of TV Show"
    by Eva Hamilton in Medford *Mail Tribune,* Sept. 30, 1973
"D'Autremont Reminiscences in Hospital" by Mary Greiner
    Kelly, in Medford *Mail Tribune*, Mar. 16, 1959
"The Murders at Tunnel 13," in Seattle Division, Postal
    Inspection Service, *Newsletter*, No. 11-73, U.S. Postal
    Service, May 23, 1973
"Murder on the Gold Special" by Jack Pement in *Oregon
    Journal* [a 12 part serial appearing daily starting]
    Sept. 25, 1973
*Picture Story of the Holdup of Southern Pacific Train
    No. 13, October 11, 1923; Capture and Conviction of
    the DeAutremont Brothers*. U.S. Post Office Department
    (1927)
"Posses Scour Hills for Bandits" in Medford *Mail Tribune*
    Oct. 12, 1923
"Railroad Gradient" (Sec. 62) in *Quiz on Railroads and
    Railroading*. Association of American Railroads,
    Washington, D.C. (1958)
"Sensational Train Robber Finally Off Parole" by James
    Long, in *Oregon Journal*, Nov. 17, 1972
"Siskiyous Are Full of Armed Men On Hunt" in Medford
    Mail Tribune, Oct 12, 1923

"Time Table" of Southern Pacific Western Region, issue
    of Oct. 25, 1987, SP Transportation Co. San Francisco

"Train Crew On No. 13 Are Killed" in Medford *Mail Trib-
    une,* Oct. 11, 1923
"Two Views of Killer [DeAutremont; a comparison of news-
    paper coverage and KGW-TV program], by Doug Baker,
    in *Oregon Journal*, Oct. 1, 1973
"Visits with DeAutremont Leave Memories of Sickness,
    Sadness" by Jack Pement in *Oregon Journal*, Nov. 1, 1973
Webber, Bert, *Oregon's Great Train Holdup*. YeGalleon
    (1973)
_____, *Oregon's Great Train Holdup*—Expanded
    Edition, YeGalleon (1974)
Wilson, Neill and Frank J. Taylor. *Southern Pacific;
    The Roaring Story of a Fighting Railroad*. McGraw-
    Hill. (1952)

MAPS

Major names as Medford, Ashland, Siskiyou, Hilt and the
forests of the mountains around the tunnel can best be
seen on the U. S. Dept. of Agriculture 1/2-inch = 1 mile
scale (page 35) map.

About the Authors

Although Bert and Margie Webber have co-authored several books on which both their names appear, Margie has also been a part of additional books credited only to Bert. Her role includes joint effort on field trips, some original writing, lots of editing, and plenty of typing. She is also a photo-lab technician.

Margie Webber earned a degree in nursing from the University of Washington and has worked in a variety of professional nursing positions from which she retired in 1988.

Bert Webber graduated from Whitworth College in journalism, then earned the Master of Library Science degree at the University of Portland. He taught History of the Pacific Northwst in a Spokane high school and was a librarian in Washington and in Oregon schools. Bert has photographed more subjects than he can recall and for a ten year period immediately following the Second World War supported his family as a commercial and free-lance newspaper cameraman. He maintains his own photo-lab to the present time.

Many of his articles are listed in the *Reader's Guide to Periodical Literature*. He is in *Who's Who in the West* and in *Contemporary Authors*.

In addition to his own books and articles he is called on as special consultant for such as the *Smithsonian Magazine* and has contributed several times to Time-Life and other books.

The Webber's make their home in Central Point between the railroad and I-5 freeway a few miles north of Medford. They have four children and several grand children.

Illustration Credits

ii	author collection
vi	by authors
9	U.S. Post Office Dept (USPO)
11	author collection (ac)
12	by authors
13	by authors
15	by authors (top); USPO
16	ac
17	ac
18	USPO
19	ac (top): USPO
20	USPO
21	UPSO
22	by authors
23	by authors(top); ac
25	USPO
26	USPO(top); by authors
27	by authors
28	by authors
31	by authors
33	USPO(top,center); by authors
35	ac
36	USPO
37	USPO
39	USPO
40	by authors
41	USPO
42	ac(top); USPO
44	USPO
45	USPO
46	by authors
47	USPO
48	USPO
50	USPO
51	ac(top); USPO
52	USPO
53	USPO
54	Medford *Mail Tribune*(top); ac
55	USPO
56	ac
57	USPO
61	*Oregon Journal*
63	ac
64	ac
65	ac
66	ac
67	Tam Moore
68	by authors
69	by authors
72	by authors
73	by authors
74	by authors
76	SP Transportation Co.
77	USPO
78	George W. Norman
79	George W. Norman
82	by authors
84	by authors

Index

Page numbers in *italic* are photos